I0488706

How To Draw Realistic Skulls Volume 2

Simple Guide to Drawing Skulls

How to Draw Skulls

By : Gala Publication

2

Published By :

Gala Publication

© Copyright 2015 – Gala Publication

ISBN-13: **978-1522785613**
ISBN-10: **1522785612**

Table of Contents

DEAD SKULL

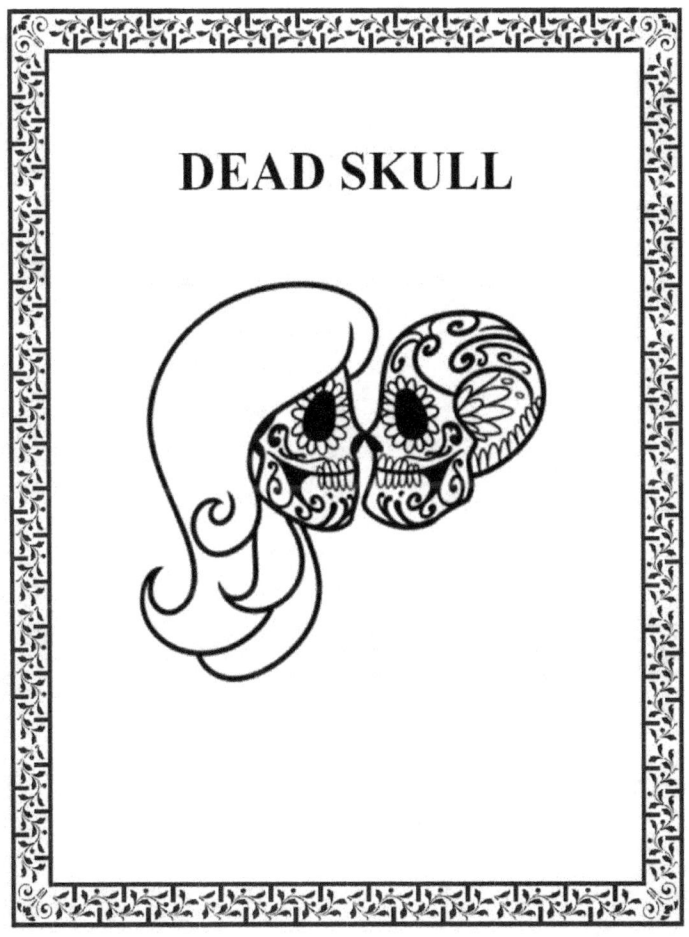

STEP 1

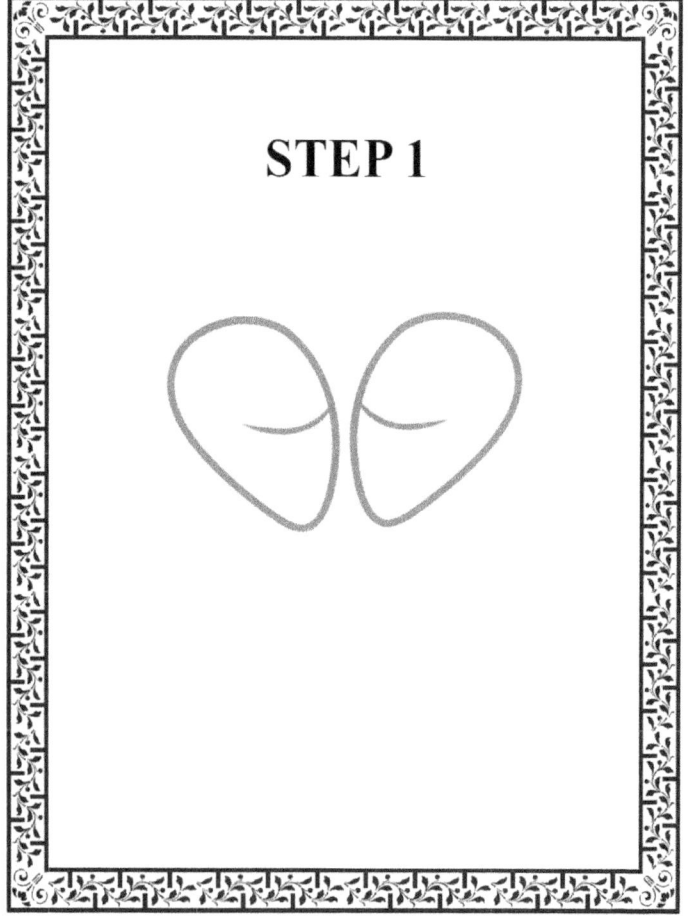

STEP 2

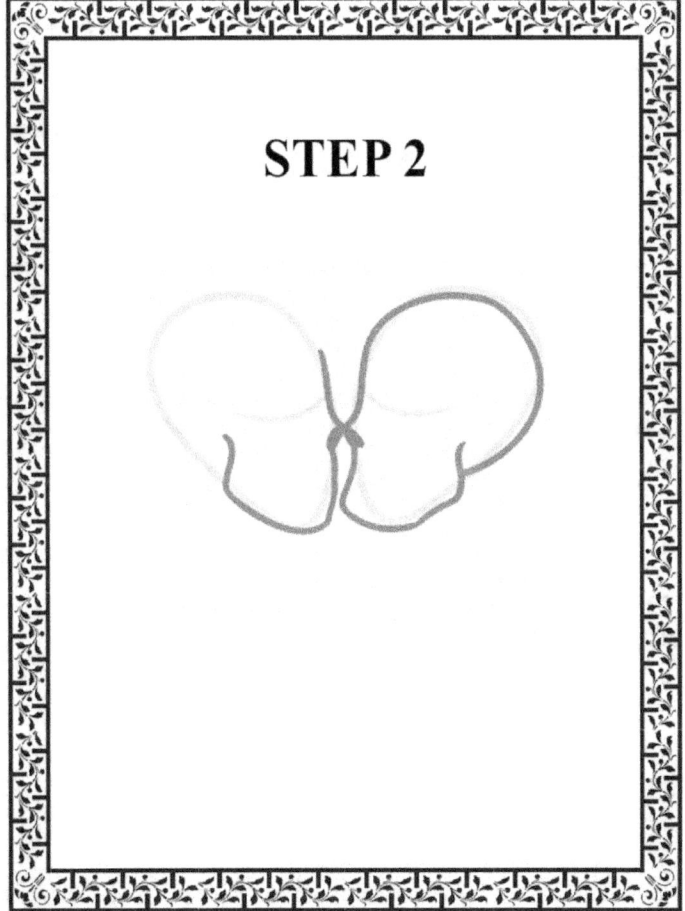

STEP 3

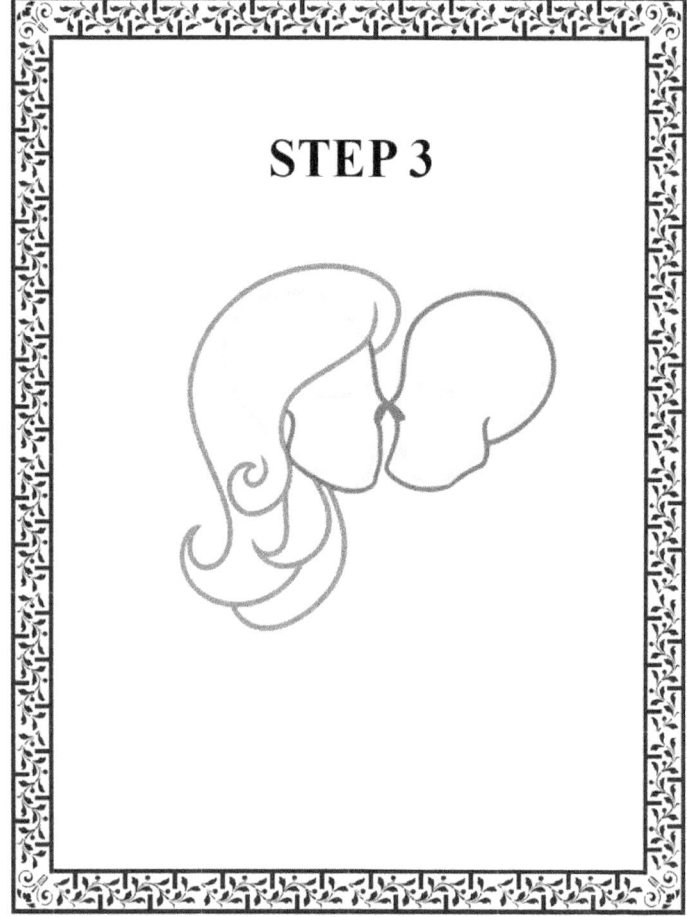

STEP 4

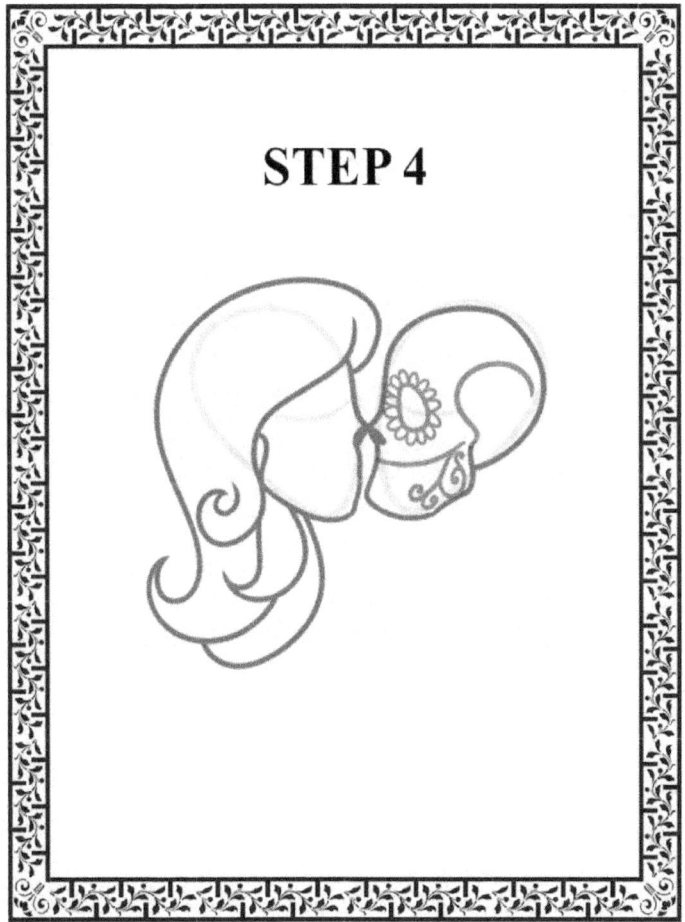

STEP 5

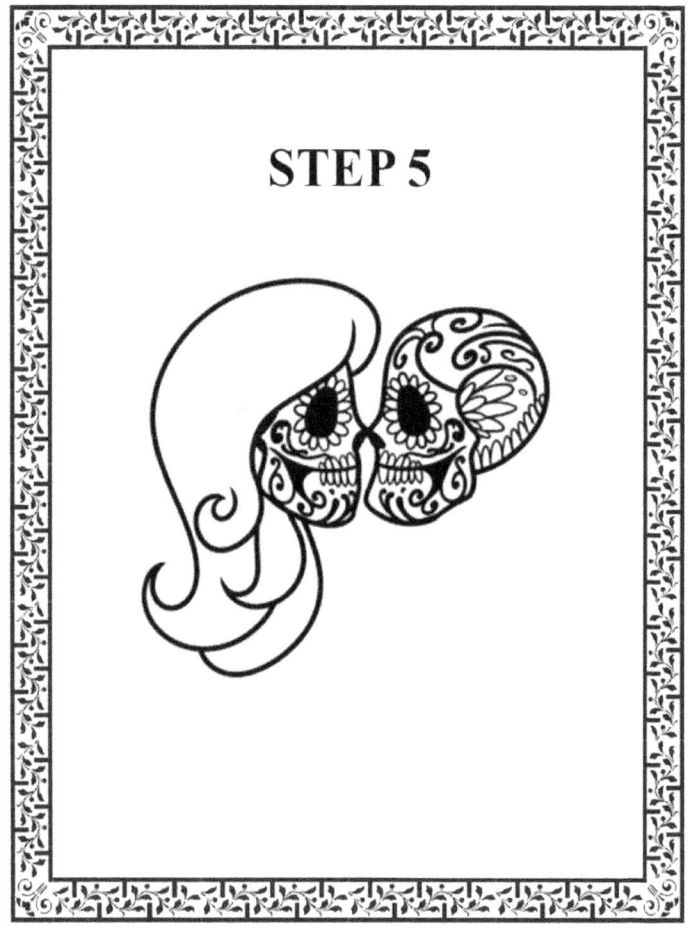

DECAYING SKULL

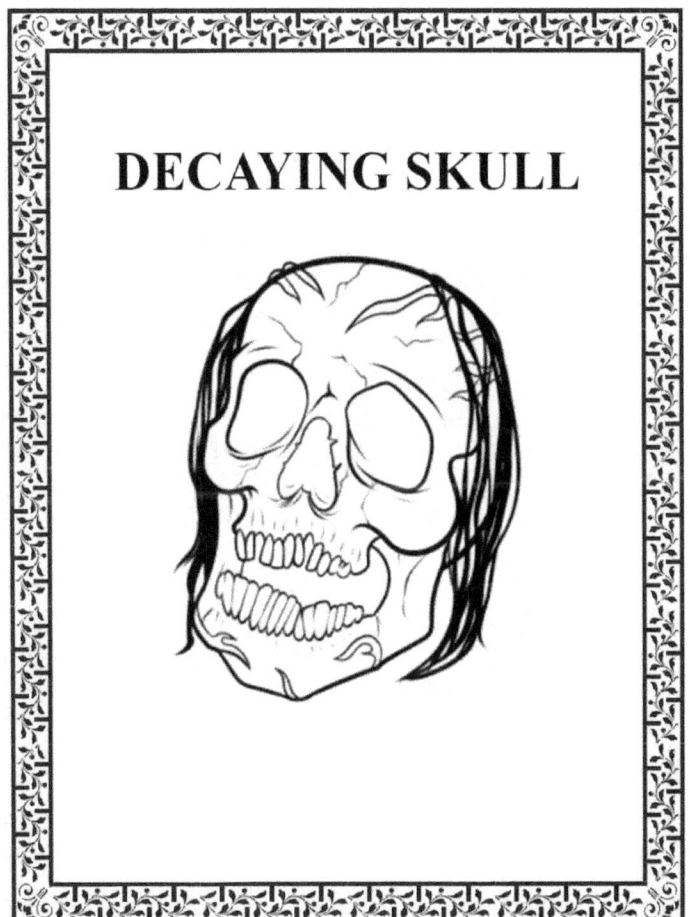

STEP 1

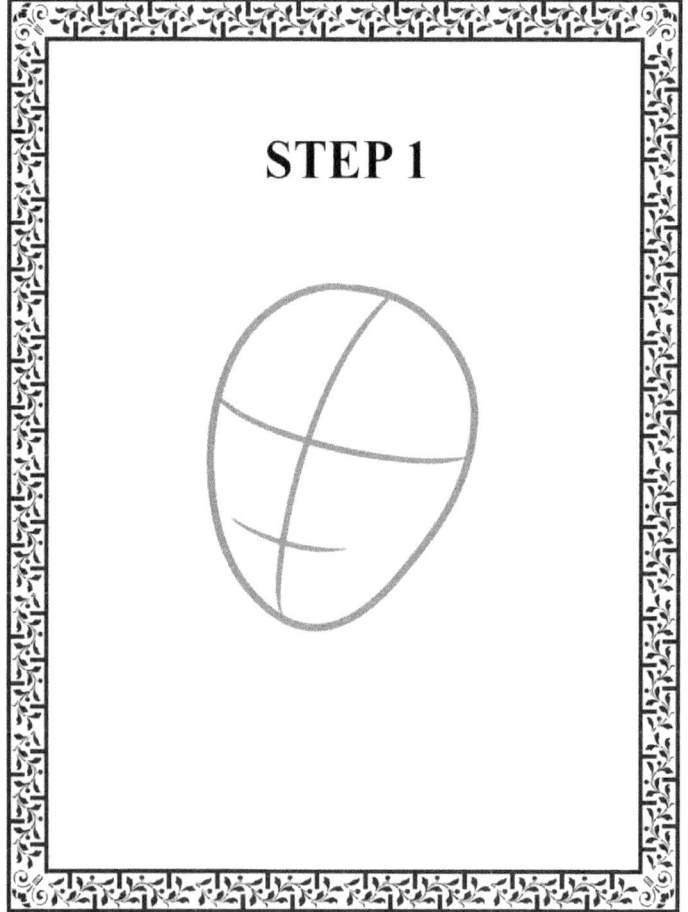

STEP 2

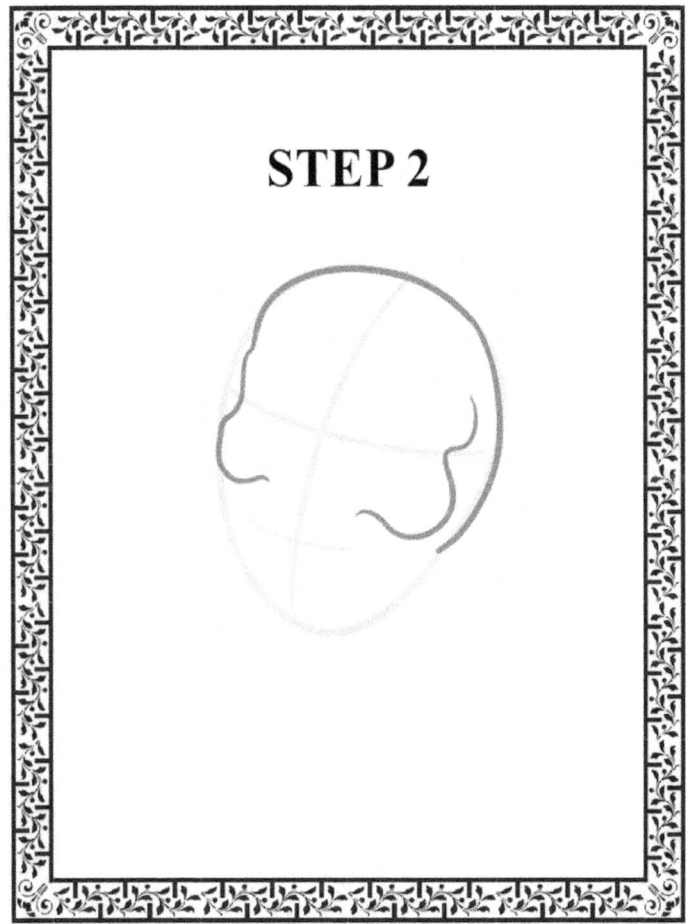

STEP 3

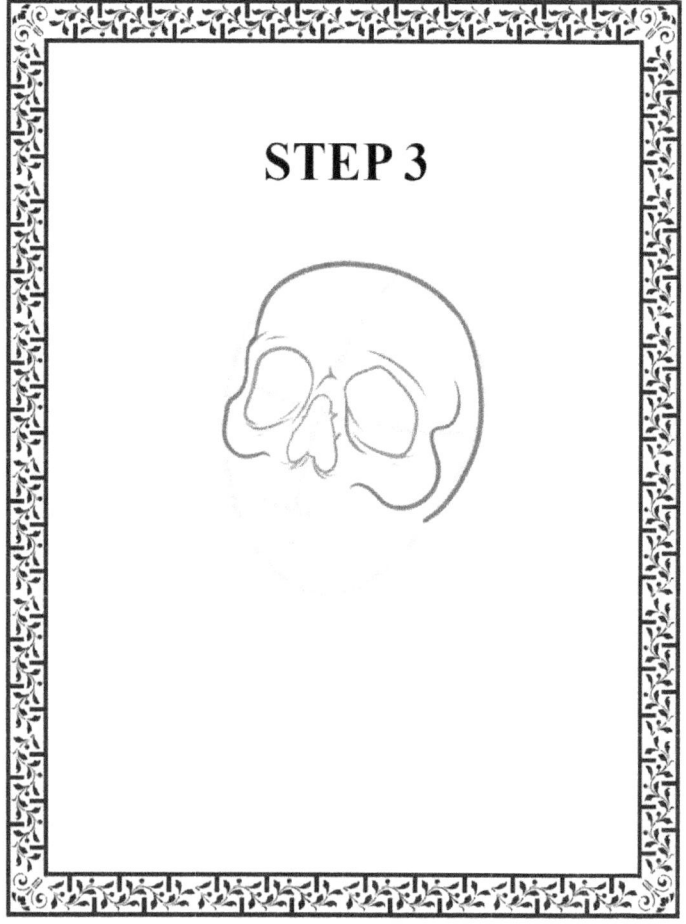

STEP 4

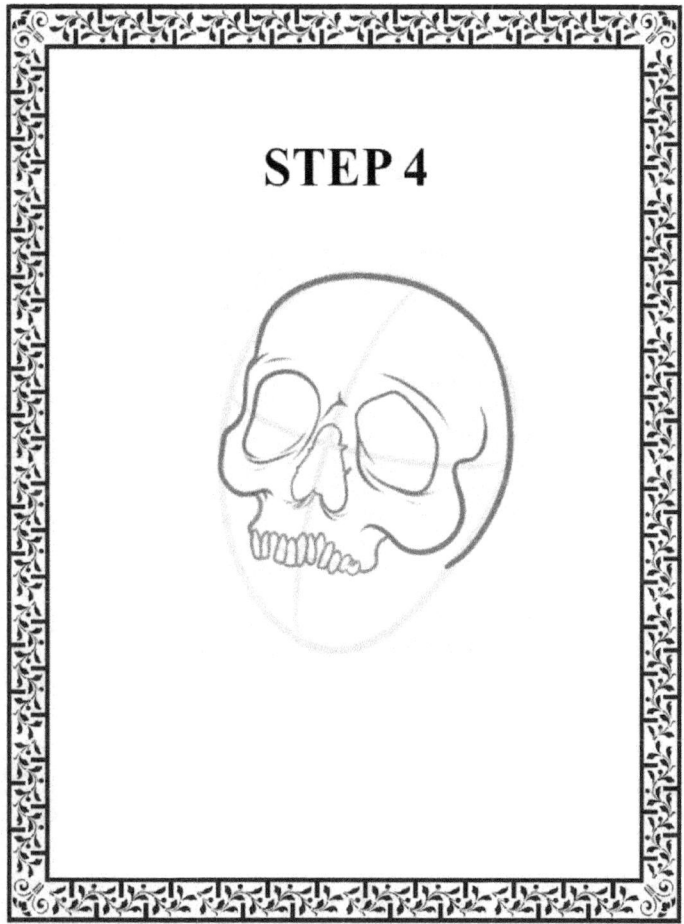

STEP 5

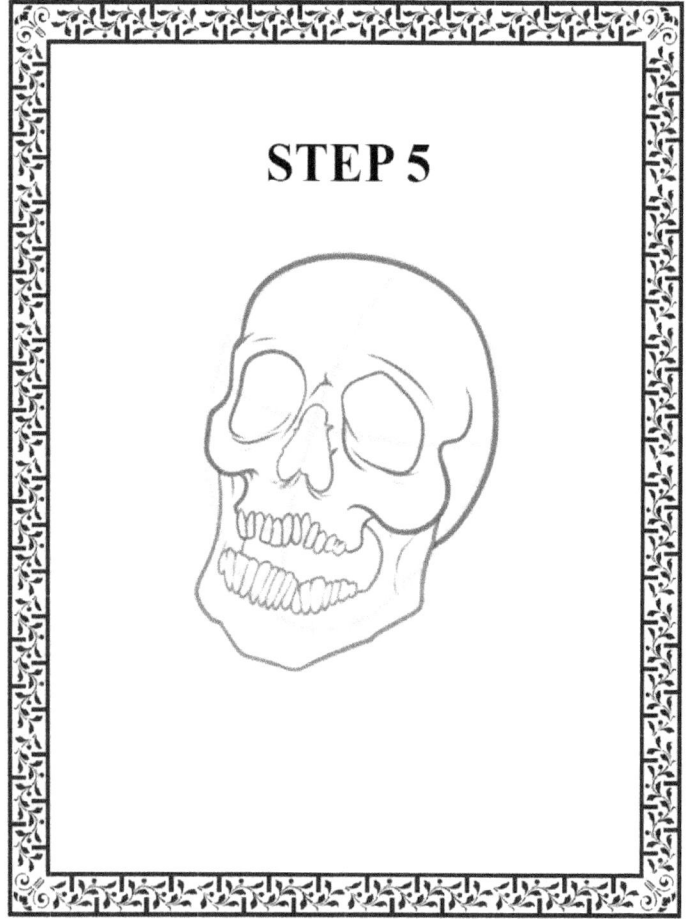

STEP 6

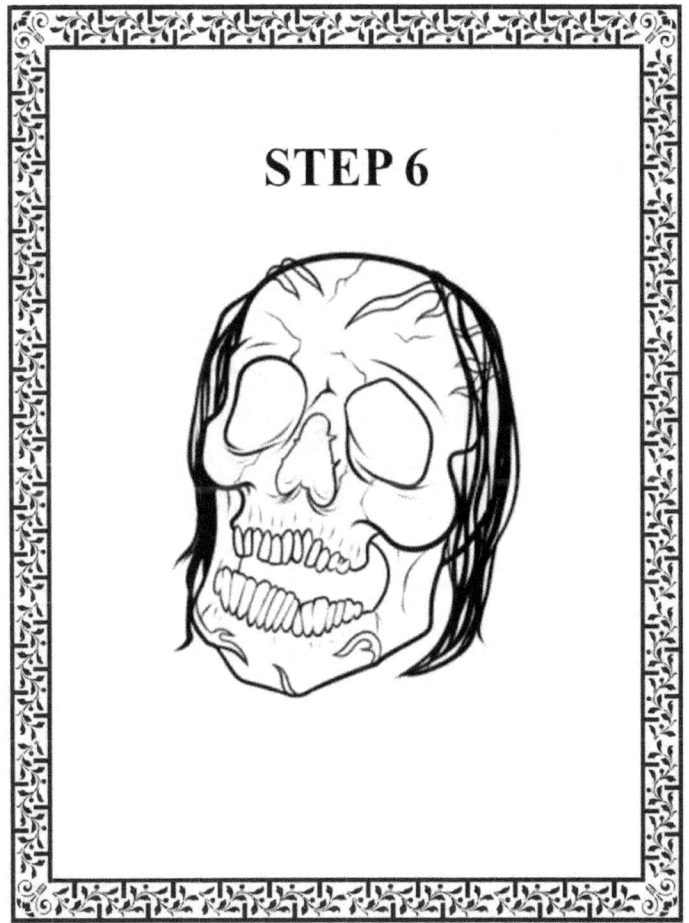

GREEN SKULL

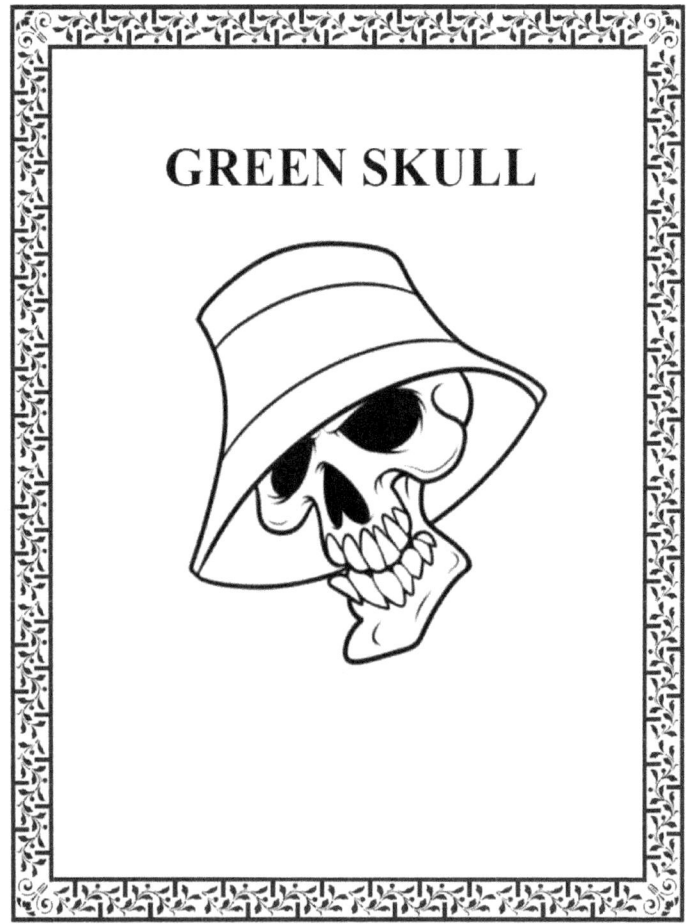

STEP 1

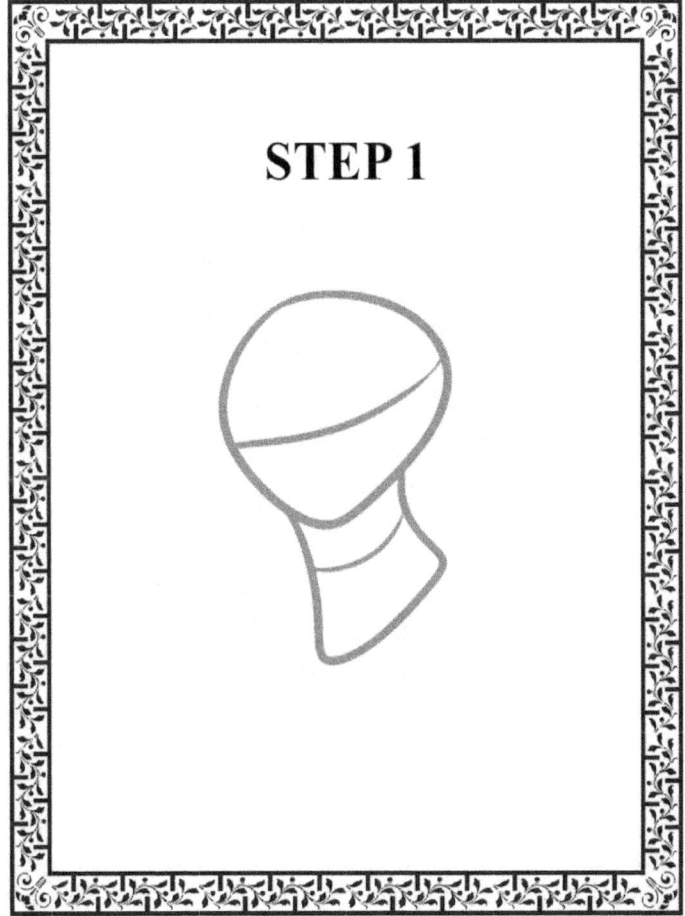

STEP 2

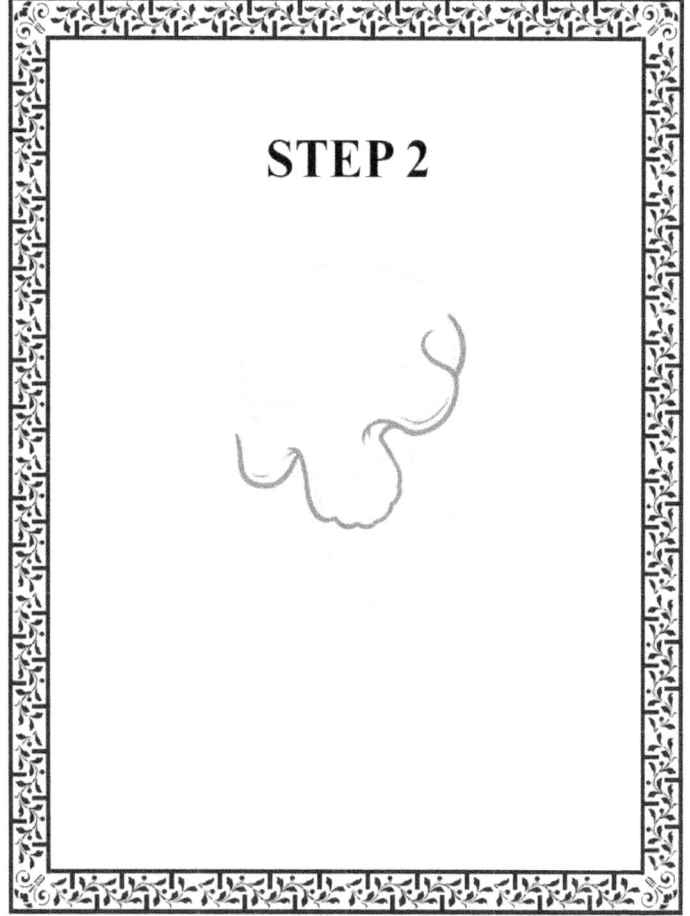

STEP 3

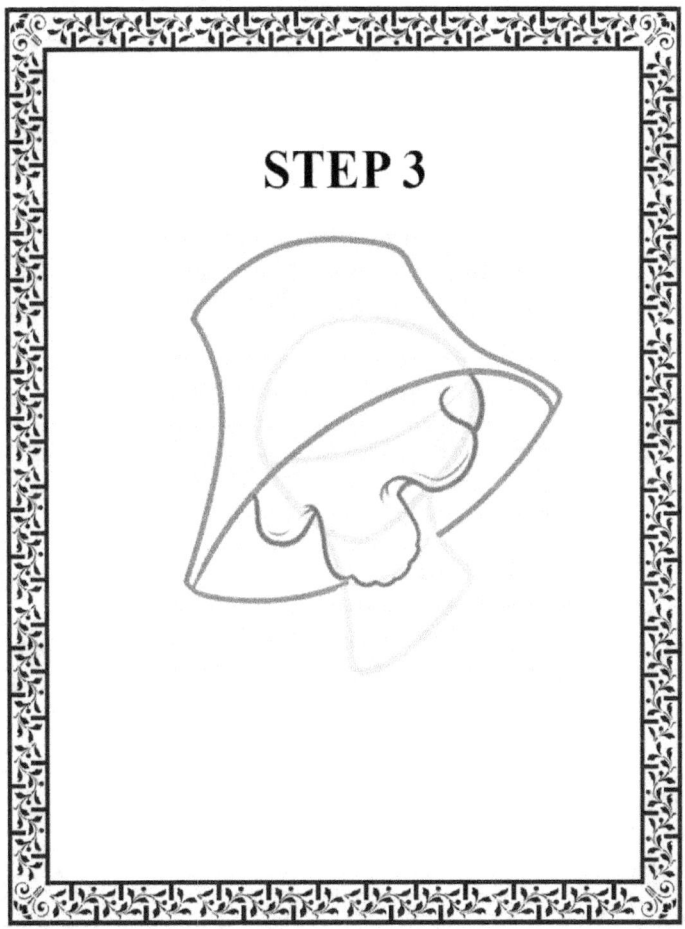

STEP 4

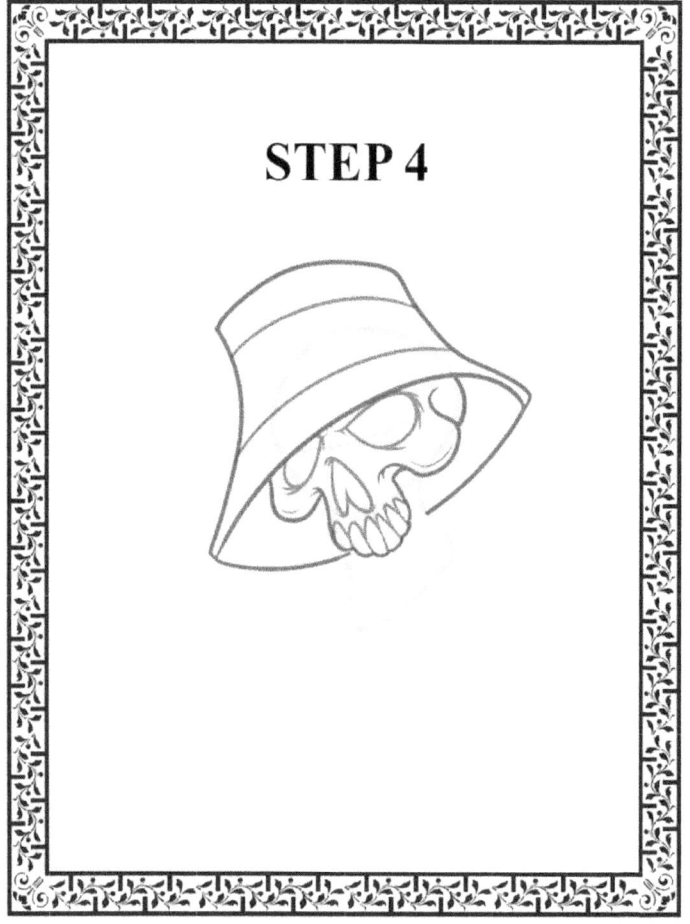

STEP 5

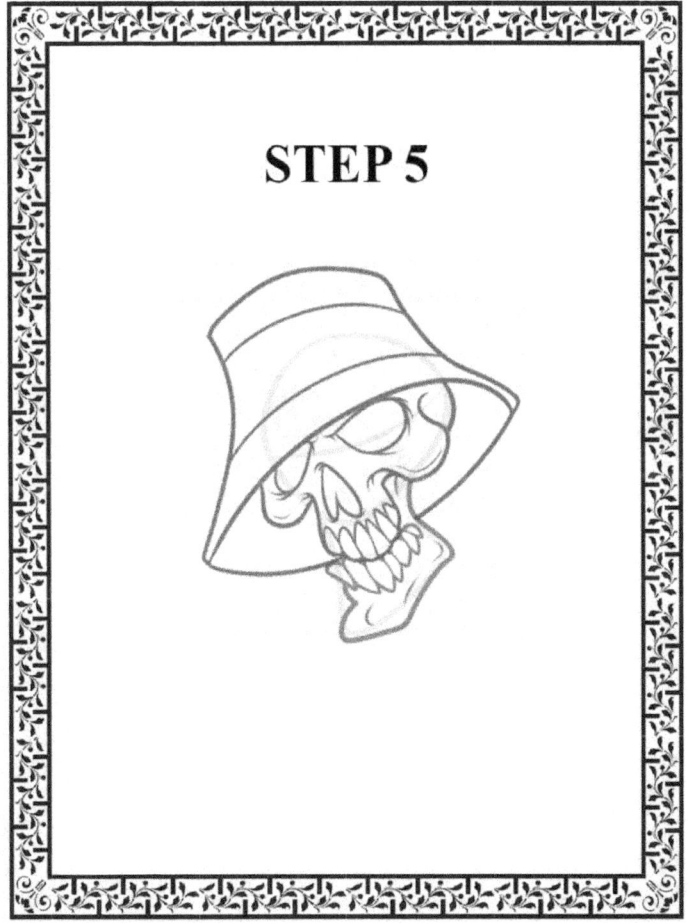

STEP 6

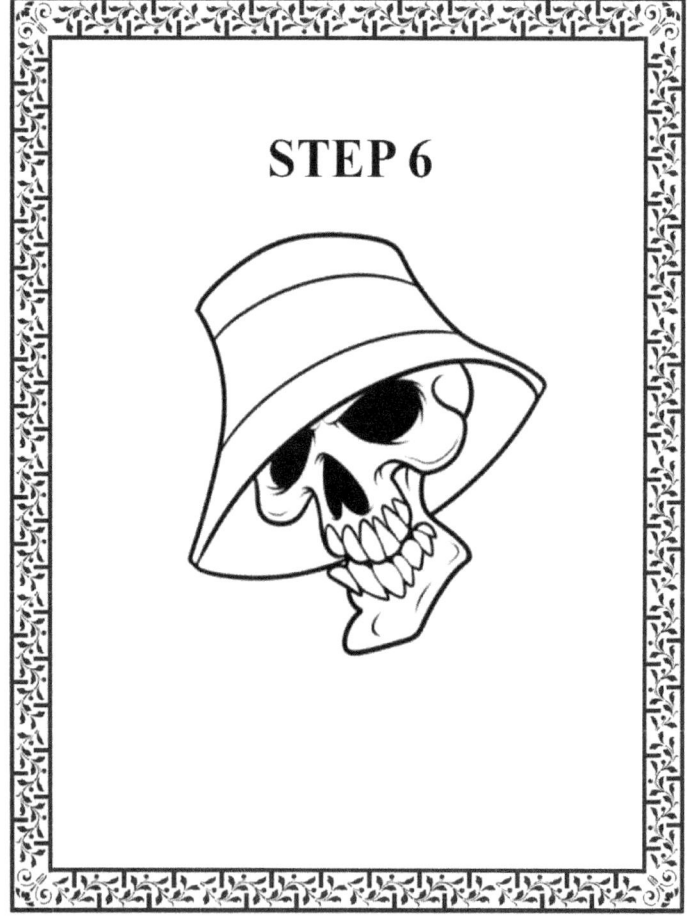

MEDIEVAL SKULL

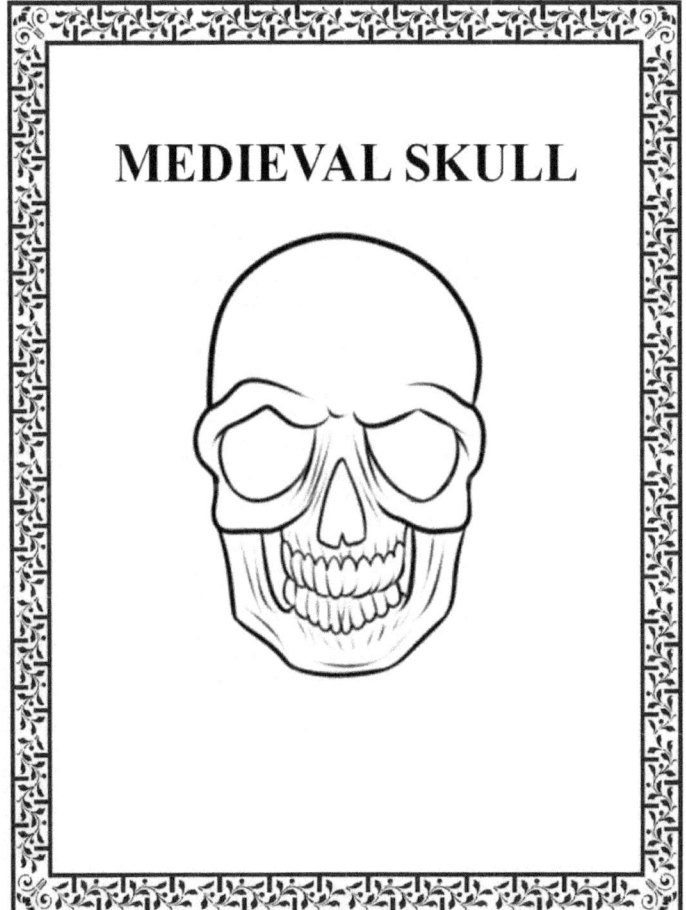

STEP 1

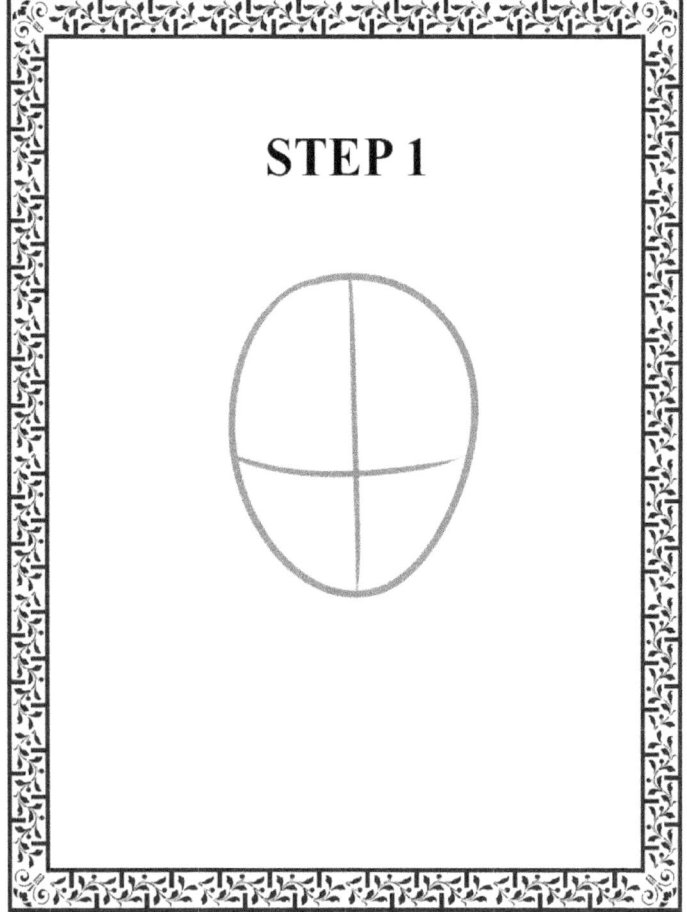

STEP 2

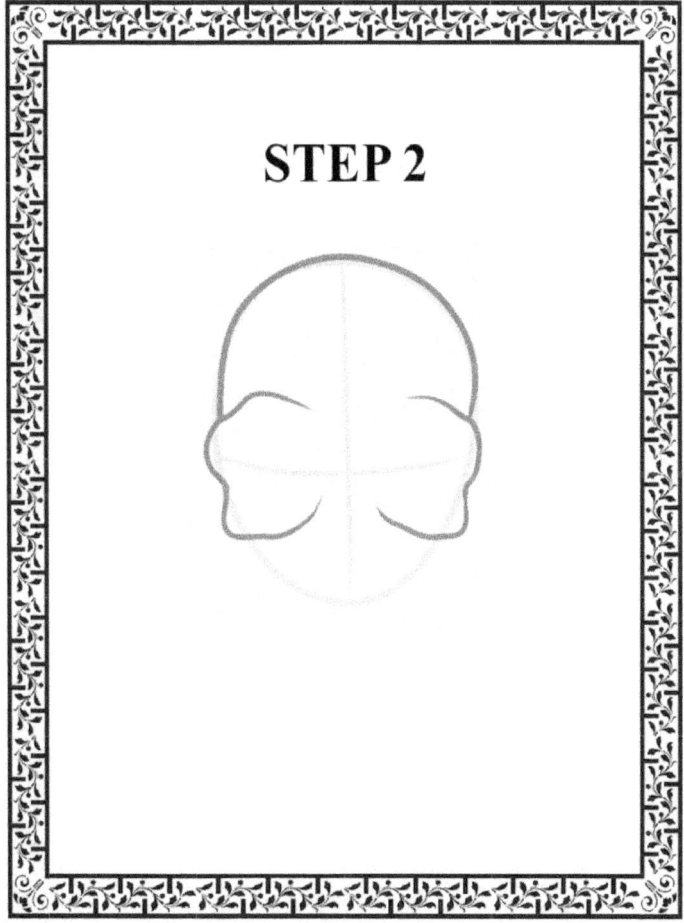

STEP 3

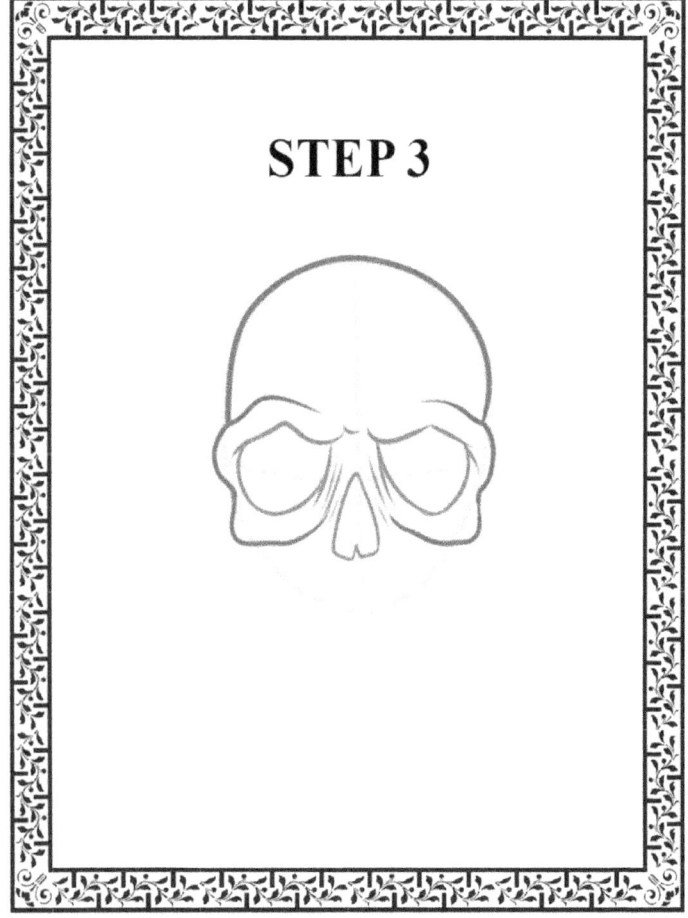

STEP 4

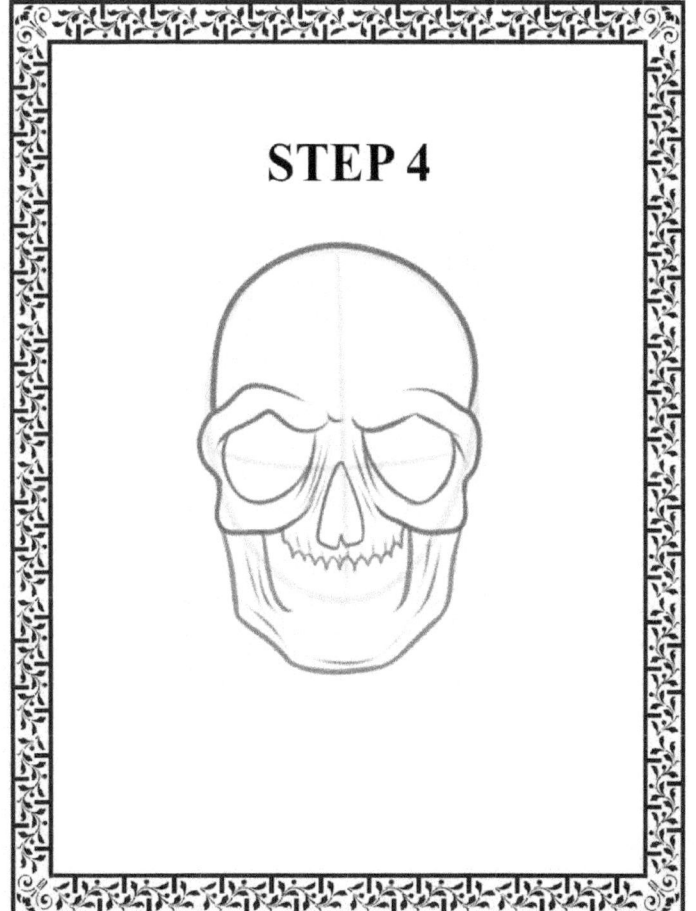

STEP 5

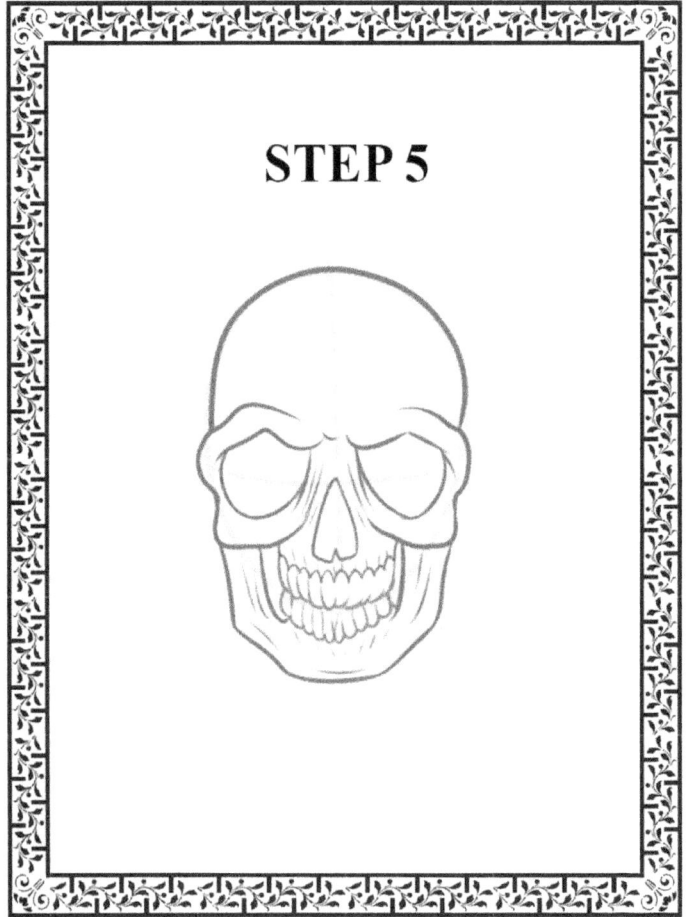

STEP 6

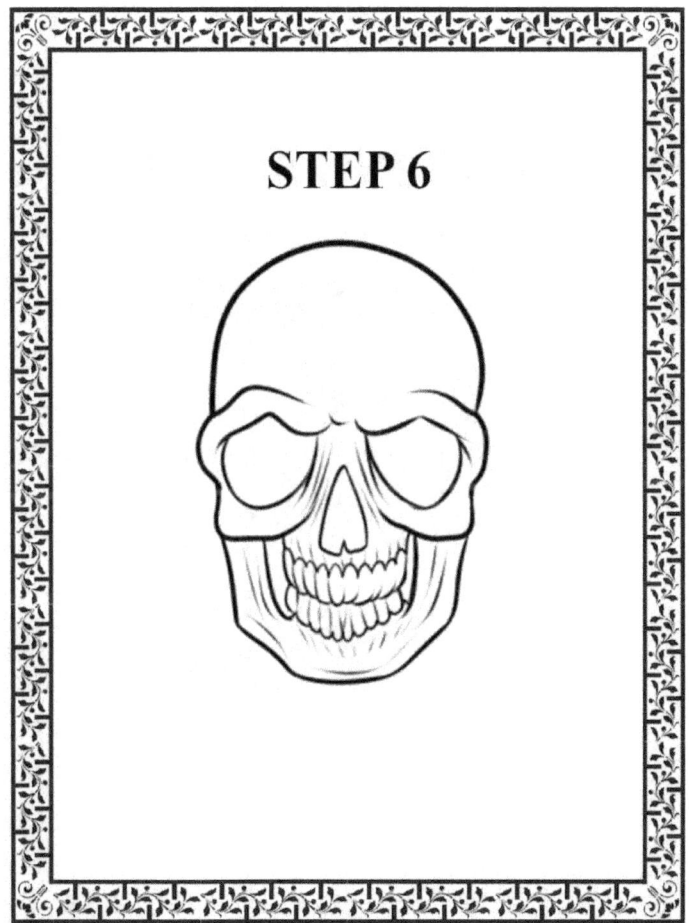

MELTING SKULL

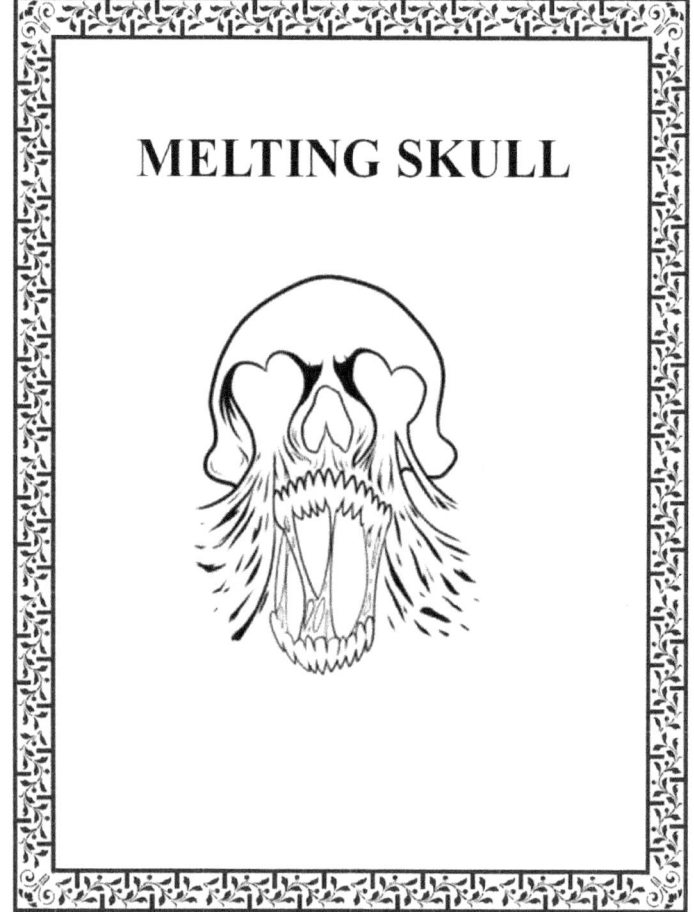

STEP 1

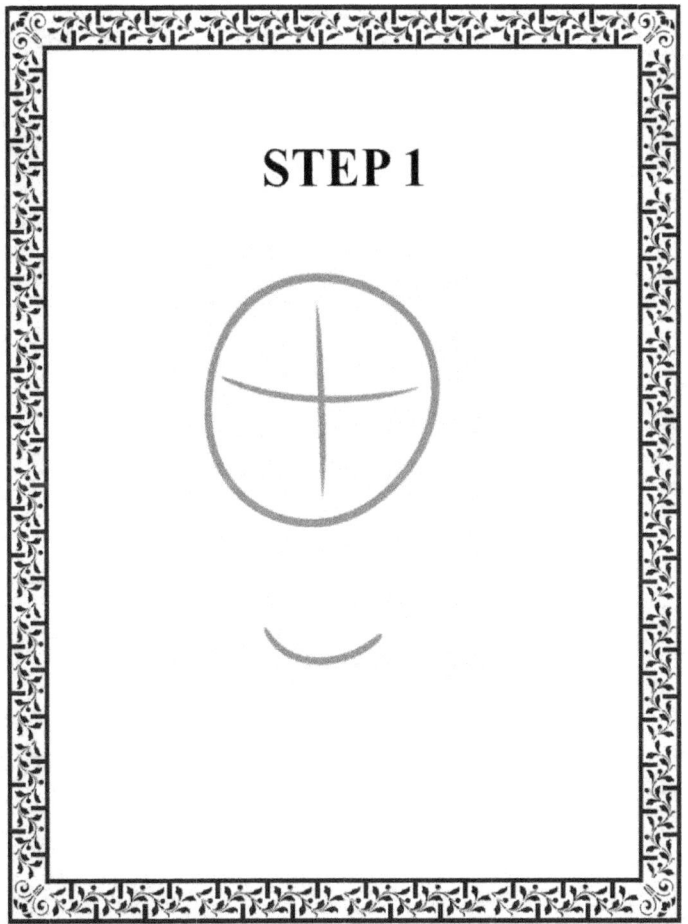

STEP 2

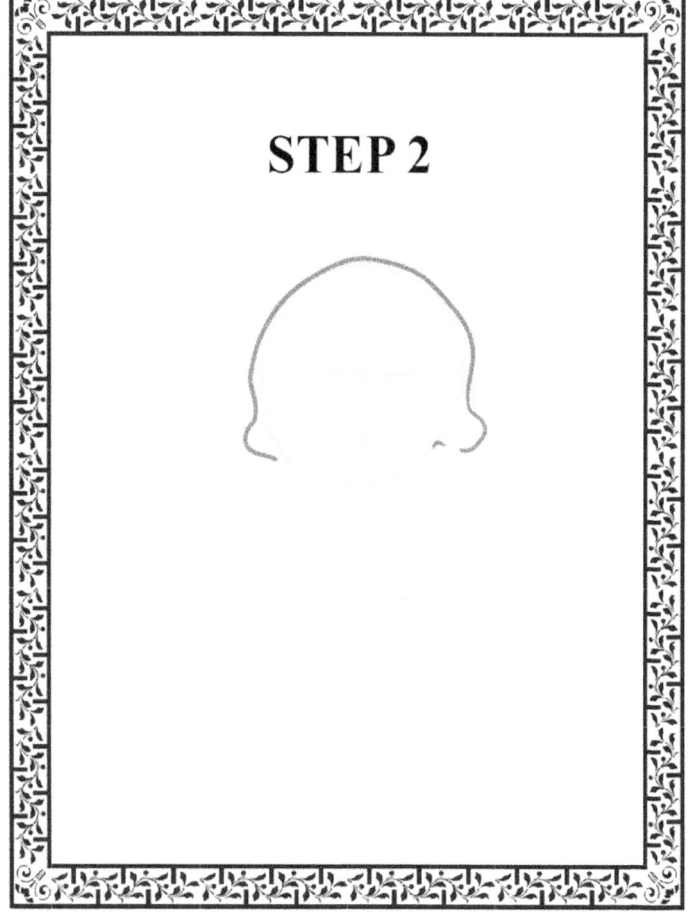

STEP 3

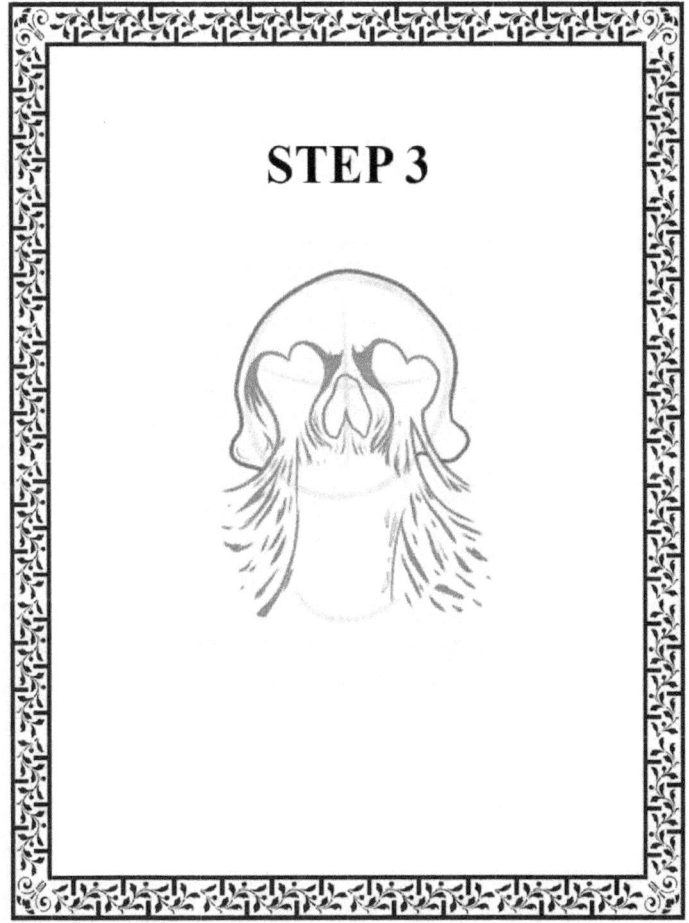

STEP 4

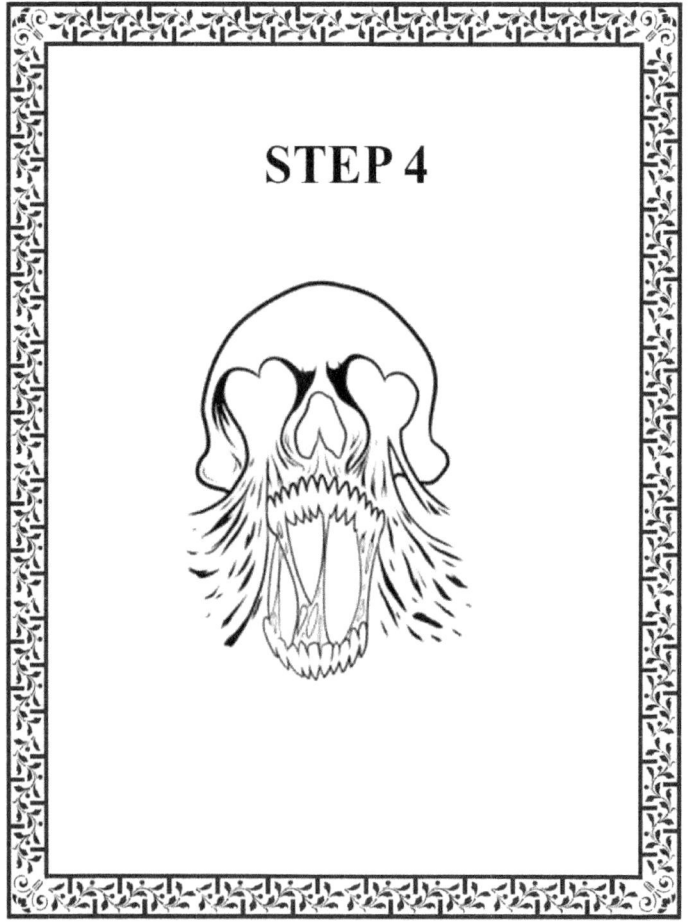

SKATER SKULL

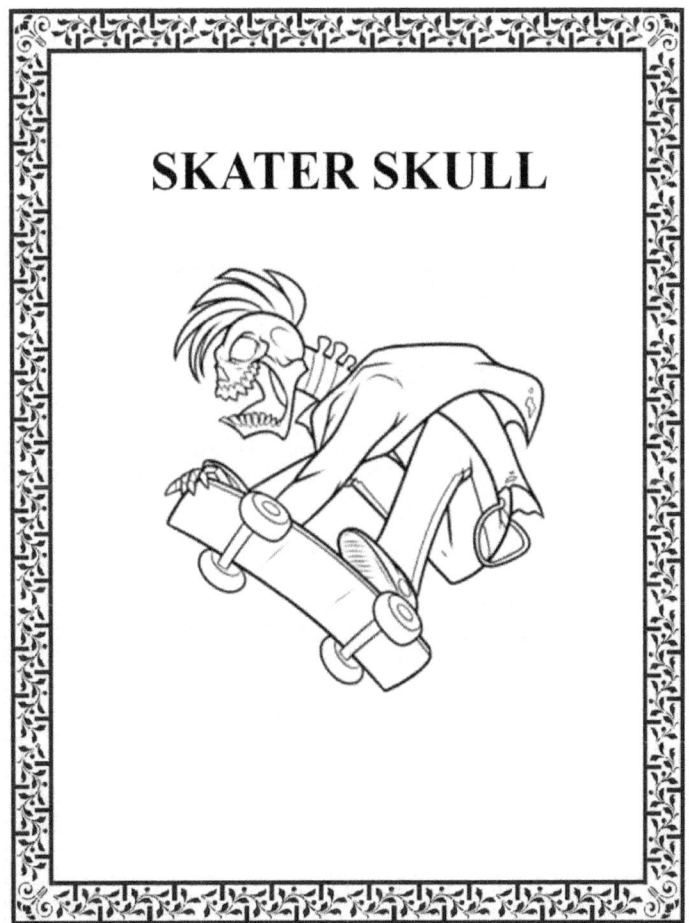

STEP 1

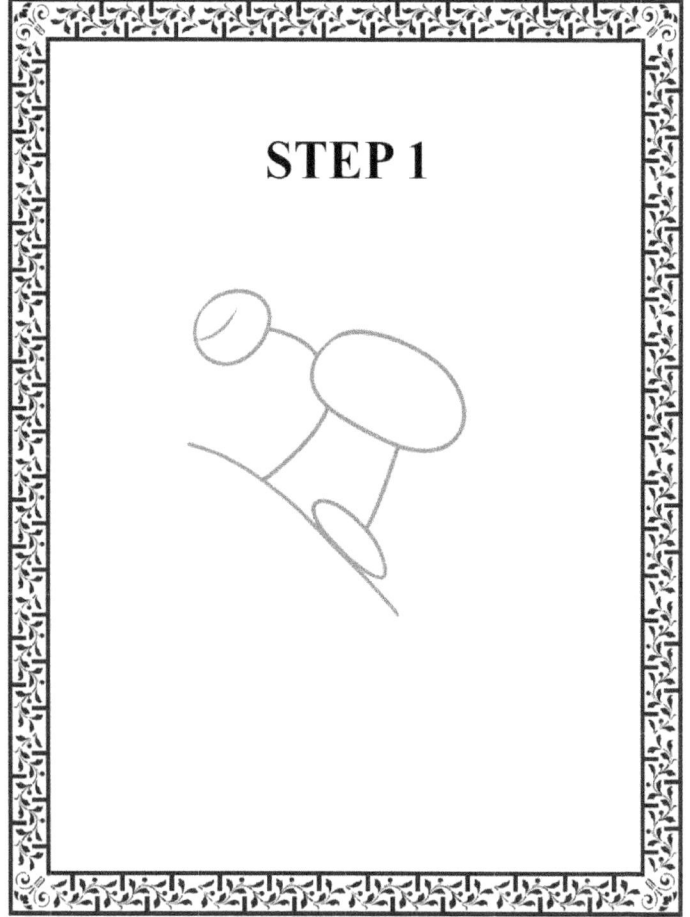

STEP 2

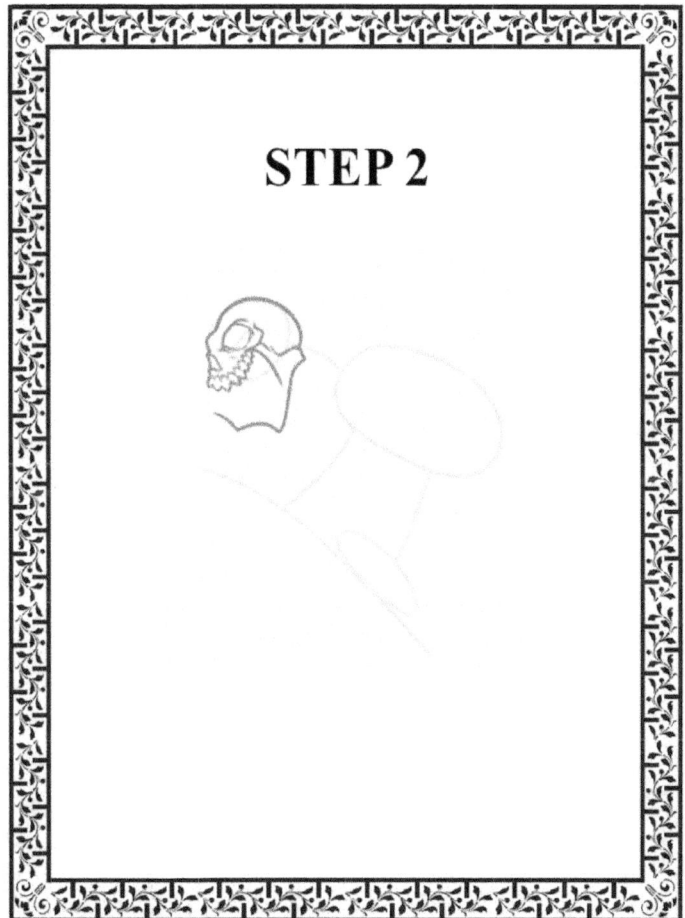

STEP 3

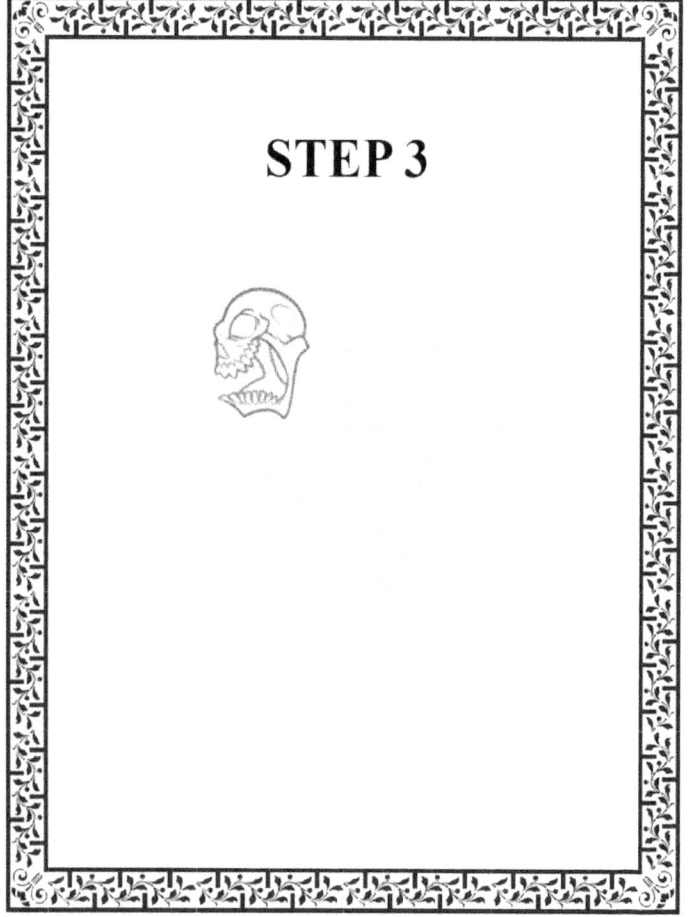

STEP 4

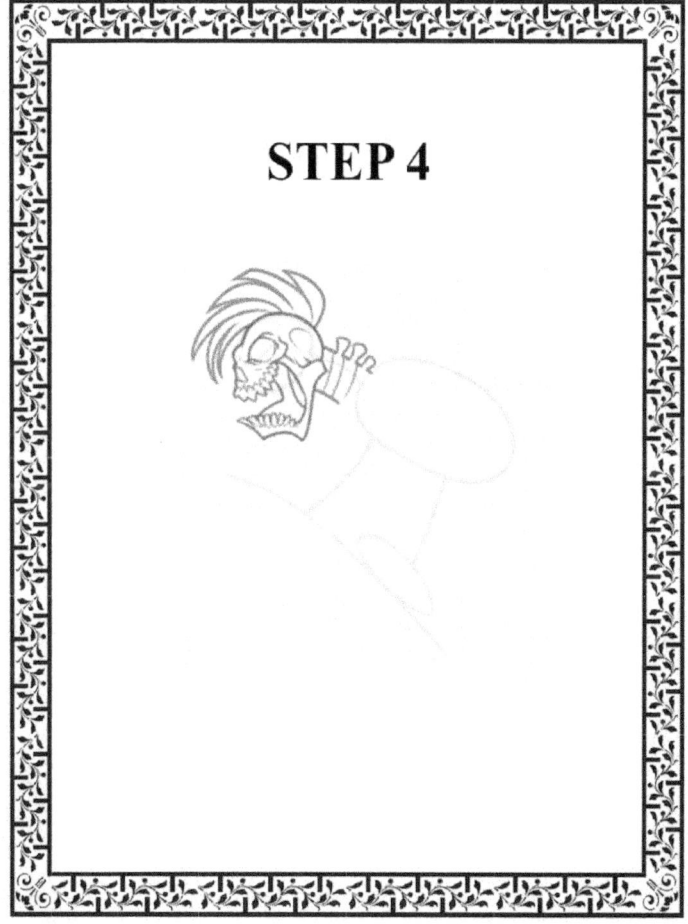

STEP 5

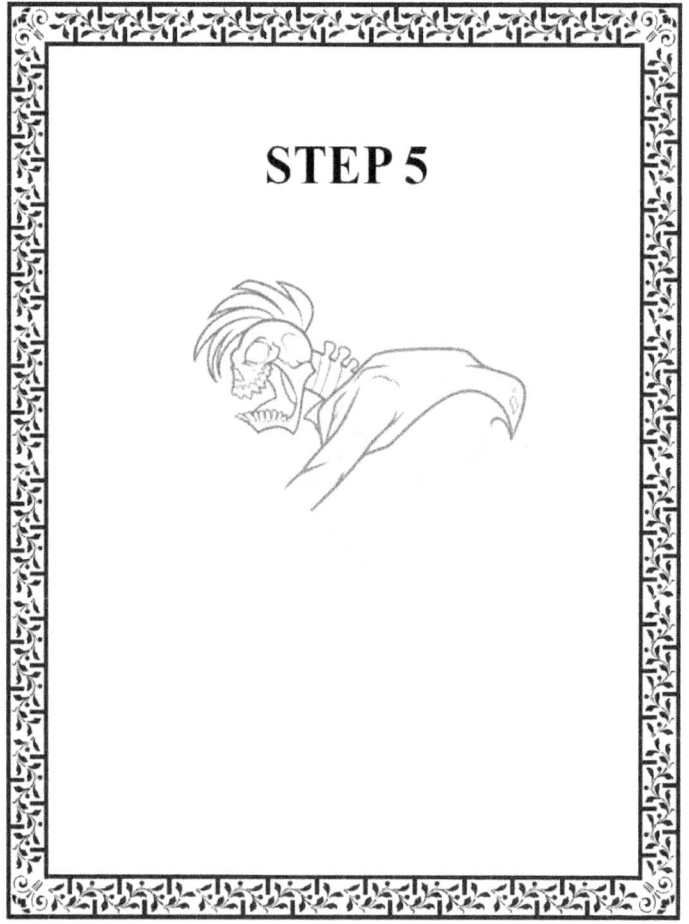

STEP 6

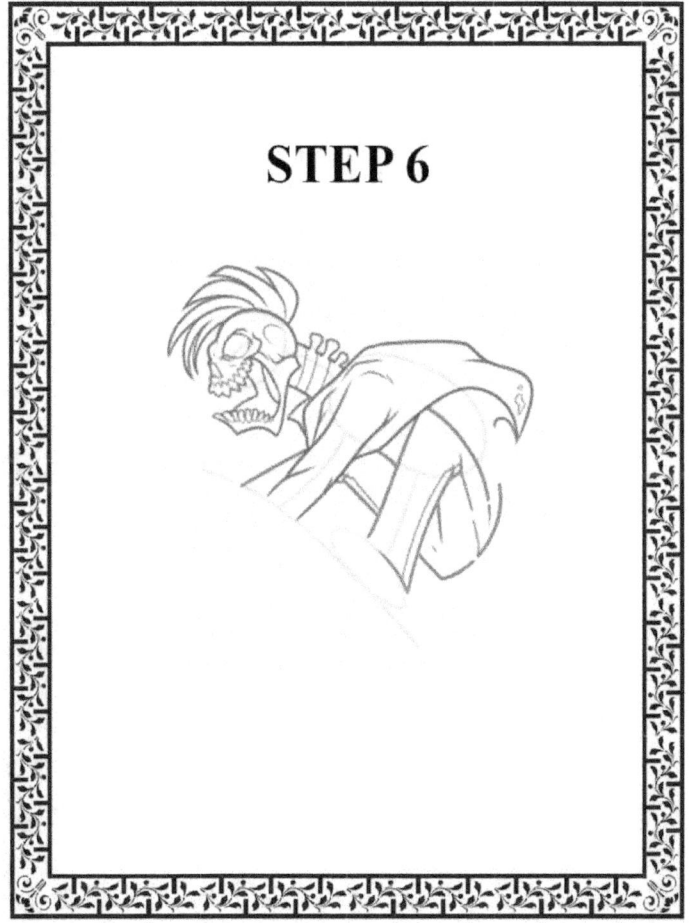

STEP 7

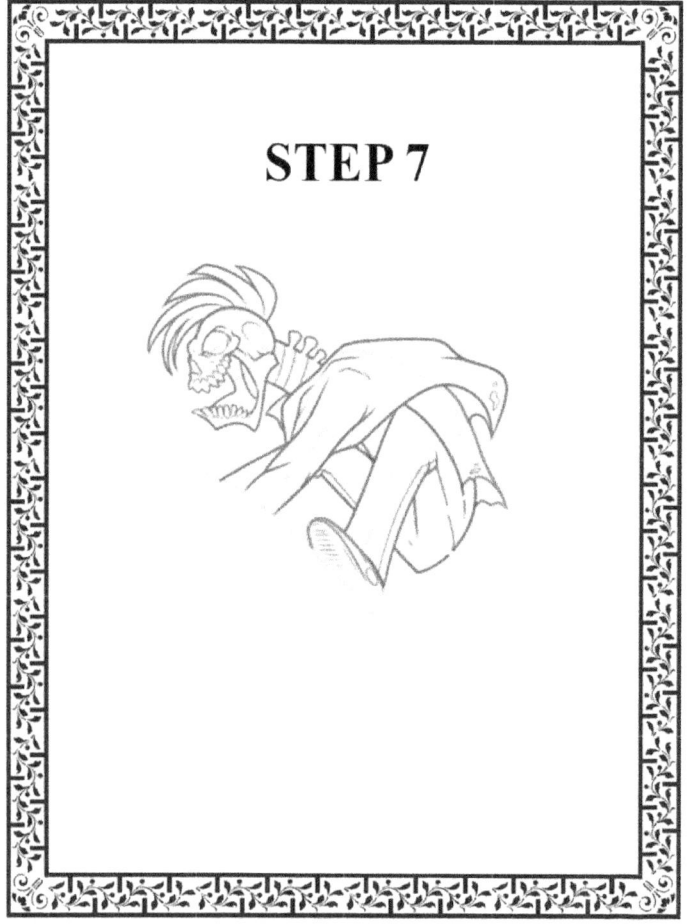

STEP 8

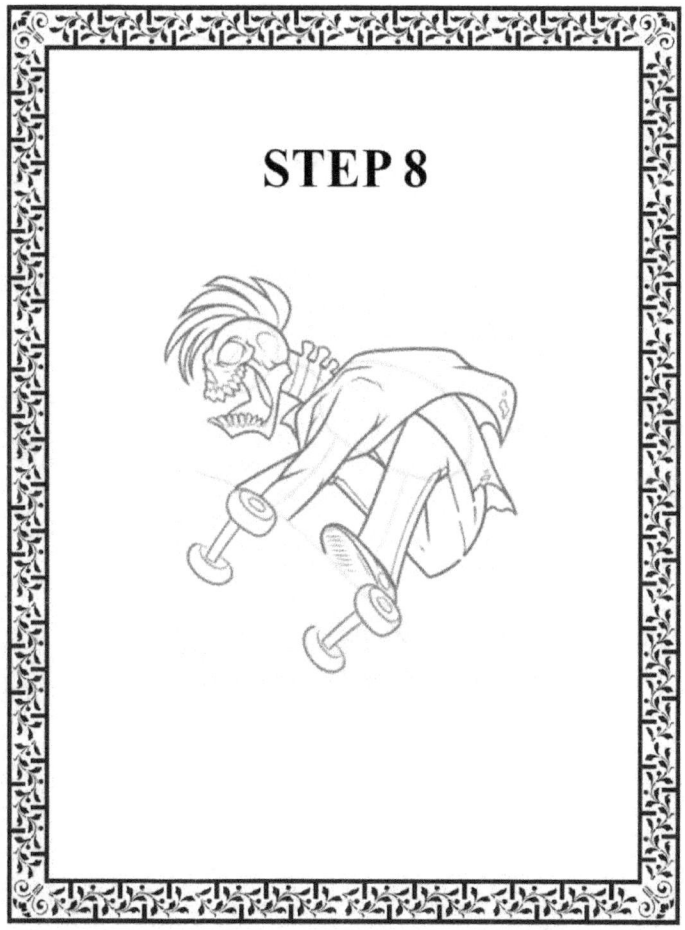

STEP 9

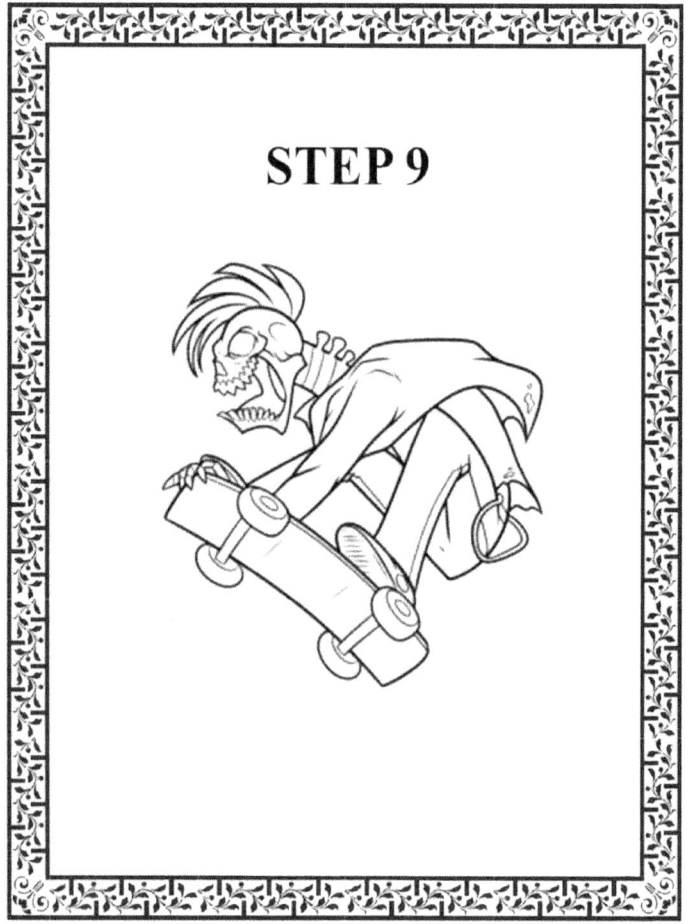